BIGGEST NAMES IN SPORTS
KEVIN DURANT
WITHDRAWN
BASKETBALL STAR

by Marty Gitlin

FOCUS READERS

WWW.NORTHSTAREDITIONS.COM

Produced for North Star Editions by Red Line Editorial.

Photographs ©: Denis Poroy/AP Images, cover, 1; Alonzo Adams/AP Images, 4–5; Larry W. Smith/EPA/Newscom, 6; Seth Poppel/Yearbook Library, 8–9; Eric Gay/AP Images, 11; Frank Franklin II/AP Images, 13; Ty Russell/AP Images, 14–15; Mark Duncan/AP Images, 17; PRNewsFoto/Kevin Durant Charity Foundation/AP Images, 18–19; John Shearer/Invision/AP Images, 21; Rick Bowmer/AP Images, 22–23; Sue Ogrocki/AP Images, 24; Shopland/BPI/Rex Features/AP Images, 27; Red Line Editorial, 29

ISBN
978-1-63517-040-5 (hardcover)
978-1-63517-096-2 (paperback)
978-1-63517-198-3 (ebook pdf)
978-1-63517-148-8 (hosted ebook)

Library of Congress Control Number: 2016951012

Printed in the United States of America
Mankato, MN
August, 2017

ABOUT THE AUTHOR

Marty Gitlin is a sportswriter and educational book author based in Cleveland, Ohio. He has had more than 100 books published, including dozens about famous athletes.

TABLE OF CONTENTS

CHAPTER 1

Breakout Game 5

CHAPTER 2

Greatness in the Making 9

CHAPTER 3

Moving Up 15

CHAPTER 4

Giving Back 19

CHAPTER 5

Shooting for the Top 23

At-a-Glance Map • 28
Focus on Kevin Durant • 30
Glossary • 31
To Learn More • 32
Index • 32

BREAKOUT GAME

Kevin Durant had already scored 38 points. And there was still more than half of the fourth quarter to go.

It was January 17, 2014. Durant's Oklahoma City Thunder led the Golden State Warriors 110–101. More than 18,000 Thunder fans cheered loudly.

Kevin Durant drives to the hoop against the Warriors.

Durant and Warriors guard Klay Thompson battle for a loose ball during Durant's 54-point game.

They wanted to see their team's star forward put the Warriors away.

Durant drained a long three-pointer. He sank another one 30 seconds later. He hit yet another with five minutes left in the game.

The Warriors were finished. But Durant was not. He scored another basket to give him 11 points in less than two minutes. And while he was hitting two **free throws** to finish the game with a career-high 54 points, the home fans began to chant: "MVP! MVP! MVP!"

Their wishes came true. Durant was indeed named Most Valuable Player (MVP) of the National Basketball Association (NBA) that season. He had led the league in scoring, averaging 32.0 points per game. Then he led the Thunder to the Western Conference finals. The MVP trophy was just icing on the cake.

MONTROSE
21
MONTROSE
3
CHRISTIAN
MONTROSE
1
CHRISTIAN
MONTROSE
5

CHAPTER 2

GREATNESS IN THE MAKING

Kevin Durant was raised by his mother and grandmother in Washington, DC. They didn't have a lot of money. But Kevin had basketball. He spent hours practicing his skills at the Seat Pleasant Recreation Center. He often ate and even slept there. He became so skilled that one day a stranger gave him a huge compliment.

Kevin (back row, center) attended Montrose Christian as a senior.

She told Kevin that he played like Michael Jordan, who was perhaps the greatest basketball player ever.

That was when Kevin began to understand his gift. He worked harder than ever. He sprinted up and down a

MOTHER KNOWS BEST

Kevin's mother was the subject of a television movie titled *The Real MVP: The Wanda Durant Story*. The title was taken from Kevin's own words about his mother after he won the MVP award in 2014. During his acceptance speech, he pointed out his mother in the audience and said, "You sacrificed for us. You're the real MVP." The film aired on the Lifetime Network in 2016. It highlighted her dedication in raising Kevin and his siblings.

Durant gives a hug to "the real MVP," his mother and most loyal fan, Wanda.

steep hill near his home until his legs gave out. He practiced his jump shot, his **rebounding**, and his drives to the basket. He competed against his talented older brother, Tony, to improve his intensity.

Kevin also got help from a local coach and **mentor**, Taras Brown. He had Kevin constantly working on his skills rather than playing **pickup games** with his buddies. Brown helped Kevin build strength and **stamina** in addition to working on his basketball skills.

Kevin got so good that he started on the varsity team as a freshman in high school. As a junior, he enrolled at basketball power Oak Hill Academy. He averaged nearly 20 points and 9 rebounds, leading Oak Hill to a 34–2 record. He then scored 23.6 points per game as a senior at Montrose Christian.

Kevin decided to take his talents to Austin, Texas, for college.

People told Kevin that he was already talented enough to play in the NBA. But the league does not allow players to join right out of high school. So he went to the University of Texas. He would be starring in the NBA soon enough.

CHAPTER 3

MOVING UP

K evin Durant was almost a complete player when he arrived in Austin, Texas. His jump shot was accurate. He used his strength and quickness to grab rebounds. He was an accurate passer. He could steal the ball and block shots. And he worked hard on defense.

Durant made quite an impression during his one season of college hoops.

Durant had just turned 18 that fall. Although he was young, he was the best player in college basketball. He averaged 25.8 points and 11.1 rebounds per game that year. Durant was the first freshman ever named Associated Press Player of the Year.

There was nothing more for Durant to prove in college. He entered the 2008 NBA **draft**. The Seattle SuperSonics took him with the second pick. The skinny 19-year-old needed time to adjust to competing against the best players in the world. But Durant quickly found his stride and ended up winning the NBA Rookie of the Year Award.

LeBron James (left) squares off with Durant during a 2008 game in Cleveland.

The team moved to Oklahoma City after Durant's first season. Thunder fans welcomed Durant and his teammates. He averaged 25.3 points in his first year there. The team was still losing. But Durant would soon lead a remarkable turnaround.

CHAPTER 4

GIVING BACK

Basketball had provided Kevin Durant with fame and fortune. But he wanted to use those advantages to help others. He had come from a poor neighborhood. He knew how important it was to give struggling children support so they could realize their **potential**.

Durant meets a boy who donated 80 pairs of shoes to flood victims.

In 2014 he launched the Kevin Durant Charity Foundation to assist at-risk youth. The organization works to keep kids healthy in body and mind. It also works to make sure children have homes to live in.

Durant understood how playing basketball had allowed him to escape poverty. So he launched the "Build It and They Will Ball" program in 2015. Its mission was to build and install beautiful basketball courts in poor neighborhoods.

He also used his wealth to help those who had suffered through natural disasters. He donated $1 million to the American Red Cross in 2013. The money

Durant was named best male athlete at the 2014 Kids' Choice Sports Awards.

assisted Oklahoma families who had lost homes and loved ones in a tornado.

Durant knew that helping people bounce back from such tragedies was far more important than basketball. But he also knew that turning the Thunder into NBA champions would thrill his fans. So he worked to make that happen.

CHAPTER 5

SHOOTING FOR THE TOP

Kevin Durant was already an NBA superstar in 2009 as he began his third season in the league. But being a superstar didn't mean much to him. He could only enjoy his greatness if his team won. And his teams had been awful in his first two years.

Durant helped turn the Thunder into a playoff team.

Durant holds the Western Conference championship trophy after leading the Thunder past San Antonio.

Durant stepped up his game. He led the NBA in scoring three straight seasons. He improved his passing, rebounding, and defense. The Thunder emerged as one of the best teams in the NBA.

They made the **playoffs** in the 2009–10 season. They won their division and two playoff rounds in 2010–11. And they took the next step in 2011–12 when they met the San Antonio Spurs in the Western Conference finals. The Thunder lost the first two games of the series, but then they won three in a row. All they needed was one more win to reach the NBA Finals. Durant finished with 34 points, 14 rebounds, and 5 **assists** in a comeback victory to win the series.

Oklahoma City went on to play the Miami Heat in the NBA Finals. The Thunder lost the series, but Durant had his team knocking on the door.

But despite their talent, Durant could not lead the Thunder back to the Finals. So in 2016, he made a difficult decision. He signed a contract with the Golden State Warriors. Thunder fans were angry. They wanted him to stay and keep trying to bring a title to Oklahoma City. Even so,

OLYMPIC HERO

Durant won Olympic gold medals with the US basketball team in 2012 and 2016. He came up huge in the 2012 gold medal game against Spain, scoring 30 points and grabbing nine rebounds. The United States won the gold with a 107–100 victory. In 2016, Durant led the team in scoring with 19.4 points per game and again scored a team-high 30 points in the gold-medal game against Serbia.

Durant was one of Team USA's best players at the 2016 Olympics.

Durant knew he had to do what was best for him. That meant leaving for Oakland, California.

The decision quickly paid off. Durant and the Warriors won the 2017 NBA title. He was named NBA Finals MVP and cemented his place as one of the greatest basketball players in the world.

KEVIN DURANT

- Height: 6 feet 9 inches (206 cm)
- Weight: 240 pounds (109 kg)
- Birth date: September 29, 1988
- Birthplace: Washington, DC
- High schools: National Christian Academy, Oak Hill Academy, Montrose Christian School
- College: University of Texas, Austin, Texas (2006–07)
- NBA teams: Seattle SuperSonics (2007–08), Oklahoma City Thunder (2008–2016), Golden State Warriors, Oakland, California (2016–)
- Major awards: 2007 Associated Press Player of the Year; 2008 NBA Rookie of the Year; 2014 NBA MVP; 2017 NBA Finals MVP

Seattle

Oakland

Washington, DC

Oklahoma City

Austin

FOCUS ON
KEVIN DURANT

Write your answers on a separate piece of paper.

1. Write a letter to a friend describing what you learned in this book.

2. Durant spends a lot of his money and free time helping underprivileged children. If you were in his position, would you do the same thing? Why or why not?

3. Why didn't Durant go straight into the NBA after high school?

   A. His mother insisted that he go to college.
   B. Nobody thought he was ready to go pro.
   C. The league doesn't allow players to go from high school straight to the NBA.

4. Why did Durant leave the Oklahoma City Thunder to play for the Golden State Warriors?

   A. His charity foundation was based in Oakland.
   B. He thought he would have a better chance at winning a title.
   C. He wanted to live closer to Seattle.

Answer key on page 32.

GLOSSARY

assists
Passes that lead directly to a teammate scoring a basket.

draft
A system that allows teams to acquire new players coming into a league.

free throws
Shots from the foul line worth one point each, given to a team after one of its players has been fouled.

mentor
A trusted adviser or teacher.

pickup games
Informal games played without officials or clocks.

playoffs
A set of games played after the regular season to decide which team will be the champion.

potential
Ability to achieve success in the future.

rebounding
Controlling the ball after a missed shot.

stamina
The ability to continue working for a long time.

TO LEARN MORE

BOOKS

Ervin, Phil. *Basketball Trivia*. Minneapolis: Abdo Publishing, 2016.

Graubart, Norman D. *The Science of Basketball*. New York: PowerKids Press, 2016.

Omoth, Tyler. *Who's Who of Pro Basketball: A Guide to the Game's Greatest Players*. North Mankato, MN: Capstone Press, 2016.

NOTE TO EDUCATORS

Visit **www.focusreaders.com** to find lesson plans, activities, links, and other resources related to this title.

INDEX

American Red Cross, 20

Austin, Texas, 15

Brown, Taras, 12

Durant, Tony, 11
Durant, Wanda, 9, 10

Golden State Warriors, 5–7, 26–27

Jordan, Michael, 10

Kevin Durant Charity Foundation, 20

Miami Heat, 25
Montrose Christian, 12

Oak Hill Academy, 12
Oakland, California, 27
Oklahoma City, Oklahoma, 17, 26
Oklahoma City Thunder, 5–7, 17, 21, 23–26

Olympic Games, 26

San Antonio Spurs, 25
Seat Pleasant Recreation Center, 9
Seattle SuperSonics, 16

University of Texas, 13, 15

Washington, DC, 9

31901062907615